# America: The Original Colonies

### Katie Sharp

# Contents

Rigby®

A Harcourt Achieve Imprint

www.Rigby.com
1-800-531-5015

# Chapter 1

# A New Frontier

It's hard to imagine a time before television, computers, or video games existed. It's even harder to imagine a time before electricity, indoor plumbing, or cars, buses, and airplanes. Life in times like those must have been very different and very hard. However, it's exactly the kind of life lived by the earliest settlers in the part of the world we call the United States.

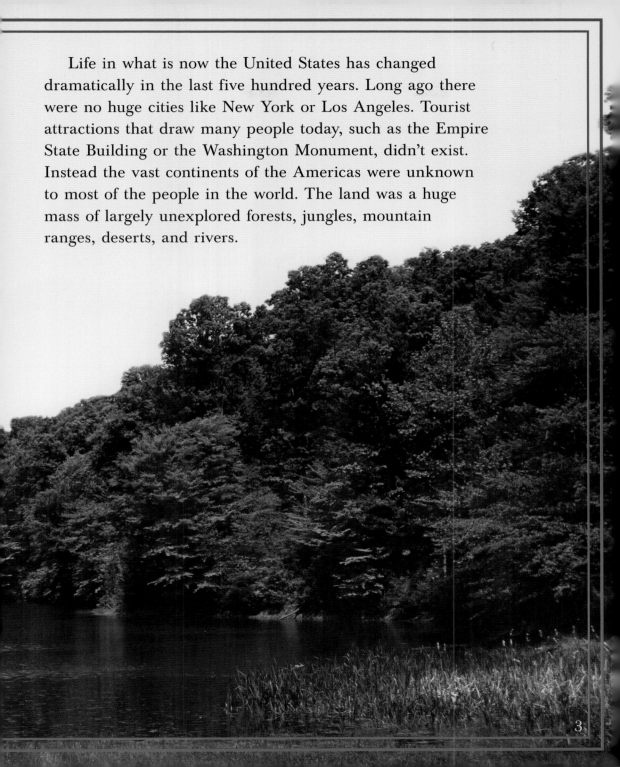

Life in what is now the United States has changed dramatically in the last five hundred years. Long ago there were no huge cities like New York or Los Angeles. Tourist attractions that draw many people today, such as the Empire State Building or the Washington Monument, didn't exist. Instead the vast continents of the Americas were unknown to most of the people in the world. The land was a huge mass of largely unexplored forests, jungles, mountain ranges, deserts, and rivers.

# Columbus Opens Up a New World

In August 1492, Christopher Columbus, an Italian explorer in command of ships paid for by the king and queen of Spain, sailed west from a Spanish port across the Atlantic Ocean. He thought he could find a more direct trade route to the Indies, what is now known as India, southeast Asia, and China. After a long and frightening journey, Columbus and his crew instead reached several islands in the Caribbean Sea. Mistakenly believing he had found a shorter route to the Indies, Columbus called the people he found living on these islands *indios*, or Indians.

Columbus returned to Europe with tales of the great wealth to be taken from these islands. He made three more voyages across the Atlantic, and as a result of his explorations, Europeans realized that Columbus had not in fact found a new route to Asia but had confirmed the existence of a "New World," the continents of North and South America.

Christopher Columbus

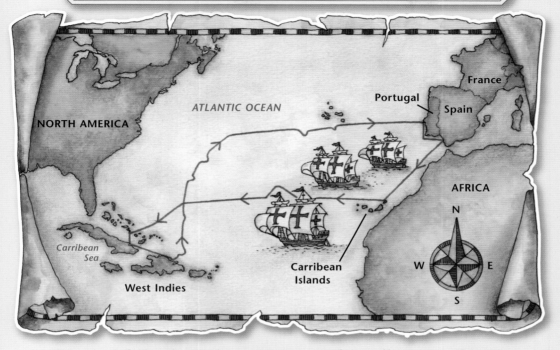

## Columbus's First Voyage to the Americas

NORTH AMERICA

ATLANTIC OCEAN

Portugal

France

Spain

AFRICA

Carribean
Sea

West Indies

Carribean
Islands

N

W　　　E

S

Word of Columbus's discoveries spread rapidly across Europe. Soon, other European countries embarked on similar **expeditions** across the Atlantic. Several different countries, including the Netherlands, Sweden, France, Portugal, and England, sent people to establish **colonies** in the New World. Europeans called the Americas the New World after Columbus's voyage because they previously thought the world consisted only of Europe, Asia, and Africa.

Some Europeans desired to travel to the Americas and settle in the newly established colonies in order to escape the laws in their home countries, which were considered by some to be harsh and unjust.

# *England Gains a Foothold in America*

Control of much of the Americas was soon divided among several European nations. By the middle of the 1600s, people from England had explored and begun to settle along the east coast of North America. The first attempt to establish an English colony in North America was at a place called Roanoke, an island off the coast of what is now North Carolina. In 1584 Sir Walter Raleigh, a close friend of Queen Elizabeth I, had received a **charter**, or legal permission, from Elizabeth to build a settlement. The first group of colonists arrived in 1585 but gave up after about a year and returned to England.

A second attempt was made in 1587. The settlers suffered many hardships and requested help from England, but difficulties prevented supply ships from reaching Roanoke until 1590. When they arrived, the sailors discovered no trace of the more than one hundred colonists. To this day, no one knows for sure what happened to the "lost colony" of Roanoke.

The English didn't completely give up, however, and eventually they established 13 colonies, from Massachusetts in the north to Georgia in the south. Different colonies were set up for different reasons: some, called **proprietary** colonies, were created to make money for investors; **royal** colonies were created at the request of the king or queen; and charter colonies were created by settlers seeking freedom to live as they chose.

# The Original 13 Colonies

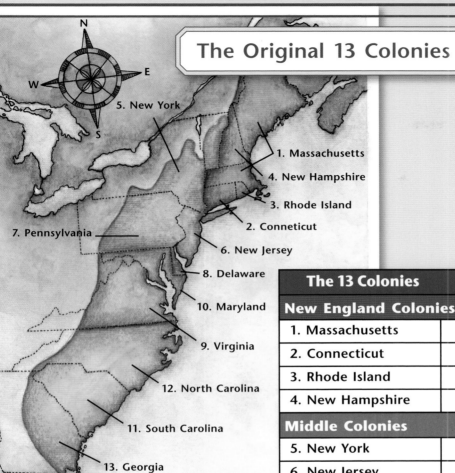

N
E
W
S

5. New York

1. Massachusetts

4. New Hampshire

3. Rhode Island

2. Conneticut

7. Pennsylvania

6. New Jersey

8. Delaware

10. Maryland

9. Virginia

12. North Carolina

11. South Carolina

13. Georgia

| The 13 Colonies | Date Founded |
|---|---|
| **New England Colonies** | |
| 1. Massachusetts | 1630 |
| 2. Connecticut | 1636 |
| 3. Rhode Island | 1647 |
| 4. New Hampshire | 1680 |
| **Middle Colonies** | |
| 5. New York | 1664 |
| 6. New Jersey | 1664 |
| 7. Pennsylvania | 1681 |
| 8. Delaware | 1638 |
| **Chesapeake Colonies** | |
| 9. Virginia | 1607 |
| 10. Maryland | 1632 |
| **Southern Colonies** | |
| 11. South Carolina | 1712 |
| 12. North Carolina | 1663 |
| 13. Georgia | 1733 |

# The New England Colonies

The shortest sea routes across the Atlantic Ocean from England led ships to the rugged northeastern coastline of North America. After a long, dangerous, and cold voyage, settlers were eager to set foot on dry land and begin working to establish a colony, even if the land they found seemed less than ideal for farming. Overjoyed at having arrived safely in America, the settlers called the Massachusetts, Connecticut, Rhode Island, and New Hampshire region New England after their homeland.

The land and climate in New England was very different from anything the settlers had known before. It was not suitable for growing certain crops because the temperatures were cold and the soil was very rocky. Over time, however, the colonists learned to grow crops from the Native Americans, such as corn, pumpkins, and squash. Since forests surrounded the area and the ocean was nearby, the colonists also learned how to hunt and fish to keep food on the table.

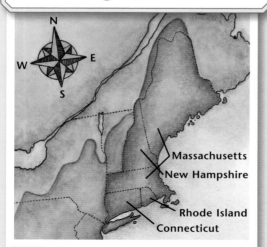

**New England Colonies**

Massachusetts
New Hampshire
Rhode Island
Connecticut

# Massachusetts

**First Settlements Established**
Plymouth: 1620
Massachusetts Bay: 1630

**Type of Colony**
Chartered

**Leaders**
William Bradford and
John Winthrop

**Did You Know?**
The name Massachusetts comes
from a Native American word that
means "the place of large hills."

Massachusetts was originally established in the 1600s as two separate colonies. The Pilgrims, who sailed to America to gain religious freedom, were the first settlers in the area and founded the colony of Plymouth. Eventually colonists settled in the area that is now Boston. The settlers named this separate colony Massachusetts Bay.

## The Pilgrims of Plymouth

In the early 1600s, English law required that all citizens be members of the Church of England. While still living in England, the people who would become the Pilgrims were known as Separatists because of their desire to practice their religion as they wished, separately from the established church. The Separatists were often jailed or fined because of their beliefs. The Separatists decided to settle in America where they could practice their religion freely.

Approximately 100 passengers boarded a ship called the *Mayflower*, which departed from Plymouth, England in September of 1620. The dreadful voyage took 66 days. There wasn't a lot of fresh air below decks, and many of the passengers got sick. However, only one person died aboard the ship.

Two months after departing from England, the *Mayflower* landed in North America. During the voyage, the Pilgrims established laws, rules, and leaders for their colony before they even set foot on the land. They called this set of laws the Mayflower Compact, and they named their settlement Plymouth in honor of their English home.

The first winter in the Plymouth Colony was difficult for the Pilgrims. They arrived too late to plant crops, and many Pilgrims died because they had little food during the winter.

Native Americans helped the early colonists to survive the harsh New England winters.

Colonists and Native Americans celebrated the first Thanksgiving together in 1622.

## Giving Thanks

Conditions improved the following spring. The Native Americans who were living in the area helped the Pilgrims in many ways. Squanto, a member of the Wampanoag tribe, stayed with the settlers. He spoke English and taught the Pilgrims how to plant corn, beans, and pumpkins. He also taught them the skills necessary to hunt and fish. During this time, William Bradford became the colony's governor.

When the next winter arrived, the colonists were living much more comfortably. They had enough food to last all winter, and they celebrated the first Thanksgiving with their Native American friends. The settlers provided the turkeys, and the Native Americans brought five deer. More and more citizens settled in the Plymouth colony over the next several years.

# The Massachusetts Bay Colony

The Puritans were another religious group who also became increasingly unhappy with the Church of England. They, too, wanted religious freedom and demanded that a new colony be established in America. King Charles I awarded the Puritans a charter to start a colony in North America, and he was happy to see them leave England.

In 1630 John Winthrop, the colony's first governor, led approximately 1,000 Puritans from England to the tiny fishing village of Salem, Massachusetts, where some separatists were already living. The religious freedom the Puritans were looking for could not be found in Salem. The Puritans were expected to attend the Separatist church services, so many of the colonists left and founded another settlement in Boston. Under the leadership of Winthrop, the Massachusetts Bay Colony grew and prospered.

John Winthrop governed the Massachusetts Bay Colony from 1629 to 1640 and from 1642 to 1649.

## Two Colonies Become One

According to the rules set forth in the colonial charter, the only colonists who could run Massachusetts Bay were men who had funded the settlements. Many settlers did not provide the settlements with financial support and were prevented from having a say in how their government was run. The settlers became angry, and eventually the colonial leaders agreed to allow the male settlers an opportunity to speak. Those in power, however, decided that only men who belonged to the Puritan church could vote on government issues.

Over time the settlers' desire for a greater voice in their own government strained the relationship between the Massachusetts Bay Colony and England. In 1684 King Charles II cancelled the colony's charter, but in 1691 a new charter was granted that combined the colonies of Plymouth and Massachusetts Bay. The unified colony was simply called Massachusetts.

Loving Cousin,
At our arrival at New Plymouth... we found all our friends and planters in good health. The Indians round about us [are] peaceable and friendly. The country [is] very pleasant and temperate, yielding...fruits. I desire your friendly care to send my wife and children to me...
Your loving kinsman,
*William Hilton*

**Letter from William Hilton**
William Hilton arrived in Plymouth in 1621. The following is part of a letter he wrote to his cousin in England.

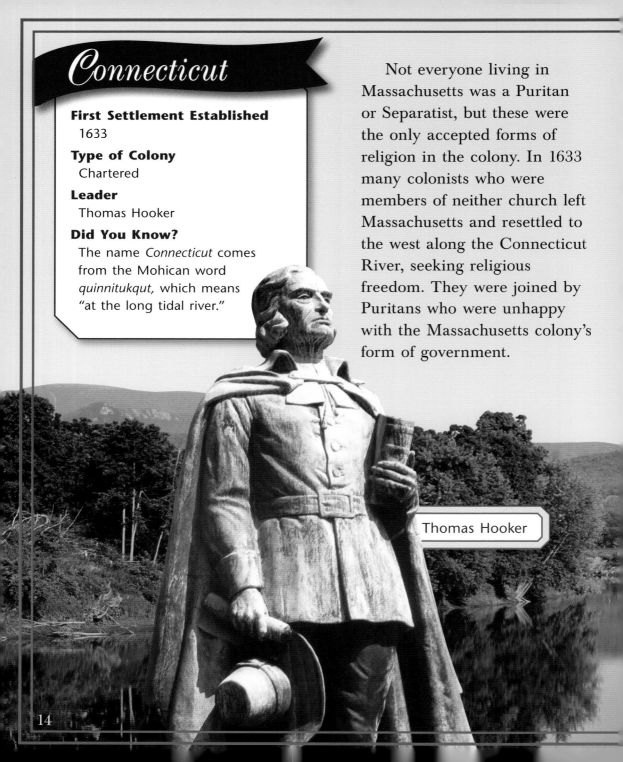

# Connecticut

**First Settlement Established**
1633

**Type of Colony**
Chartered

**Leader**
Thomas Hooker

**Did You Know?**
The name *Connecticut* comes from the Mohican word *quinnitukqut,* which means "at the long tidal river."

Not everyone living in Massachusetts was a Puritan or Separatist, but these were the only accepted forms of religion in the colony. In 1633 many colonists who were members of neither church left Massachusetts and resettled to the west along the Connecticut River, seeking religious freedom. They were joined by Puritans who were unhappy with the Massachusetts colony's form of government.

Thomas Hooker

Thomas Hooker had been a Puritan minister in the Massachusetts colony. While he practiced and supported the Puritan religion, he disagreed with the colony's government. He believed the governor and other leaders had gained too much power, and he wanted to establish a new colony with a different system of government.

In 1636 Hooker, along with approximately 100 people from the Puritan church, headed to the area that is now the state of Connecticut. They founded the settlement of Hartford along the Connecticut River. Eventually Hartford joined with other colonies in the area to form the Connecticut Colony.

Hooker helped to form Connecticut's government in 1639. He and other leaders wrote the Fundamental Orders of Connecticut. These laws gave people the right to elect members of their government.

## New Haven

John Davenport was a Massachusetts Puritan who believed the laws established in the Connecticut colony were not strict enough. In 1638 he formed a new colony, which was called New Haven. New Haven colonists created a list of laws that told people how they should behave. One law said that every male should have his hair cut a specific way.

Over the next several years, the Connecticut and New Haven colonies grew. In 1662 John Winthrop, Jr., governor of the Connecticut Colony, was recognized with a charter from the king of England. But the New Haven colony was located on the land that was assigned to Winthrop in the charter. The leaders of New Haven resisted the charter until 1664, when they rejoined the Connecticut colony.

John Davenport stablished the New Haven colony.

### Connecticut Home Schools

Education was extremely important in the Connecticut Colony. Parents wanted their children to read so they could practice their religion, and it was usually the father's job to be the teacher. By 1650 all children in the colony were required by law to learn to read as well as learn a trade or profession, such as carpentry or medicine. Children usually learned their father's trade and continued the family business.

# Rhode Island

Like Thomas Hooker, Roger Williams was a Puritan minister who disagreed with Massachusetts's government. He felt the leaders in Massachusetts were abusing their power. Williams was not afraid to voice his opinion and did not believe that England had the right to give away land in North America. Instead he believed the land belonged to the Native Americans. He also firmly believed that religion and government should be kept separate. He stated that the government's job was to establish law and order, and he believed that the government should not support any one religion.

Roger Williams felt that no one should be forced to follow a specific religion. Most Puritans disagreed with Williams. They thought telling people what to believe was the government's job.

## Williams Escapes

Williams was often in trouble with Massachusetts leaders because of his opinions. In 1635 Roger Williams was forced to leave Salem. He spent the winter with the Narragansetts, a Native American tribe.

The following spring, Williams purchased land from the Narragansetts and established Providence Plantations. The plantations were not considered a colony in the eyes of the English government because Williams had not been provided with a charter to settle the land.

## Religious Tolerance

Williams didn't think it was right to force anyone to believe as he did. Williams thought colonists should be able to practice their religion freely, no matter what their religion might be. He believed in religious **tolerance**. He also gave all white men the right to vote. In time, more and more people came to Rhode Island to enjoy this freedom.

As other settlements developed in the area, Williams finally received a charter from England in 1644. He suggested that the settlements join together and form one colony. In 1647 a single colony was established and was named Rhode Island.

The leaders of the other New England colonies often threatened to invade and take over Rhode Island. In 1663 the leaders of Rhode Island received a charter from England to prevent an invasion. This charter, which was called the Charter of Rhode Island and Providence Plantations, served as law in Rhode Island for almost 100 years. The Charter of Rhode Island and Providence Plantations established complete religious freedom, which was unique at the time.

## Anne Hutchinson

Anne Hutchinson was a Massachusetts Puritan who openly expressed her views about the church. Governor Winthrop was not happy with Hutchinson and believed she was guilty of many wrongdoings. In 1637 she was ordered to leave the colony and the Puritan church. Hutchison and her family fled to Rhode Island, where Williams helped her buy land from the Native Americans. The settlement she and others started was called Portsmouth.

# New Hampshire

**First Settlement Established**
1623

**Type of Colony**
Proprietary

**Leaders**
Ferdinando Gorges; John Mason

**Did You Know?**
New Hampshire was named after the county of Hampshire in England.

Unlike the other New England colonies, New Hampshire was not created for religious reasons. Instead it was established as a place where settlers could earn money by fishing.

In 1622 the English government gave John Mason and Sir Ferdinando Gorges permission to start a colony in an area of North America between the Merrimack and Kennebec Rivers.

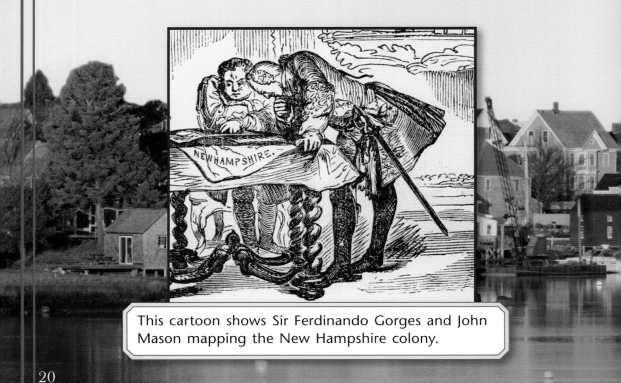

This cartoon shows Sir Ferdinando Gorges and John Mason mapping the New Hampshire colony.

Mason sent David Thomson and brothers Edward and Thomas Hilton to settle the area in 1623. He encouraged them to establish fishing villages along the Piscataqua River. Thomson began a settlement at Odiorne Point, while the Hiltons established their settlement at Dover.

## A Royal Decision

In 1629 Mason claimed the area between the Piscataqua and Merrimack Rivers. He named this land New Hampshire. Over time, New Hampshire colonists established four settlements: Dover, Portsmouth, Exeter, and Hampton.

The leaders of the Massachusetts and New Hampshire settlements continually argued over the borders between their colonies. From 1641 to 1679, the Massachusetts government attempted to control New Hampshire, but King Charles II of England settled the dispute by declaring New Hampshire a separate colony in 1680.

# Chapter 3

# The Middle Colonies

The colonies of New York, New Jersey, Pennsylvania, and Delaware were called the Middle Colonies because they were located between New England and the southern colonies.

Many colonists in this area were successful farmers who primarily grew wheat, corn, and other crops that were **exported** to Europe.

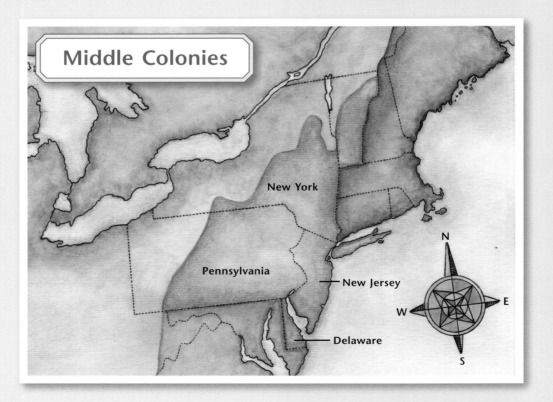

**Middle Colonies**

New York

Pennsylvania

New Jersey

Delaware

# New York

**First Settlements Established**
1624

**Type of Colony**
Proprietary

**Leaders**
Peter Minuit

**Did You Know?**
The colony of New York was eventually named in honor of James, Duke of York. He was the brother of King Charles II.

In 1609 the English explorer Henry Hudson sailed north along the river that would later bear his name—the Hudson River. Leaders from the Netherlands had hired Hudson to explore this region of North America. The Netherlands claimed all the lands that Hudson explored. The Dutch originally named this large area of land New Netherland.

Henry Hudson explored the region that eventually became New York.

# New Amsterdam

After Hudson's explorations, the Dutch established several settlements in New Netherland. The first settlement was named Fort Orange and was established in 1624. (Fort Orange was later renamed Albany.) In 1626 Peter Minuit led a group of Dutch settlers to the mouth of the Hudson River. Upon his arrival, Minuit bargained with the Native Americans living in the region to claim Manhattan Island. Reportedly, Manhattan Island was purchased for about 24 dollars worth of goods, mostly beads. Minuit called the settlement New Amsterdam.

New Amsterdam quickly became a busy port. People from various countries, religions, and backgrounds settled in the colony. Several different languages were commonly heard on the streets.

Meanwhile, English settlers from Connecticut and Massachusetts left their colonies and settled on what is today Long Island. Because this land belonged to the Dutch, the settlers were required to obey Dutch law for many years. Over time this caused a conflict between the English and Dutch, who argued over trading rights.

## Colonial Clothing

Colonists wore clothing that was very different from the clothes worn today. Most items were made from wool, linen, or leather—there weren't many comfortable cotton clothes in those days. Very young children—both girls and boys—wore long dresses that looked like nightgowns. Older boys wore long linen shirts and short wool or leather pants called breeches. Some wore waistcoats, or vests, made of wool or leather. Colonial girls and women nearly always wore long dresses and covered their hair with bonnets.

## The English Take Over

In 1664 England's King Charles II decided to seize New Netherland from the Dutch. The English were prepared to fight upon their arrival at the New Amsterdam harbor. Peter Stuyvesant, the Dutch governor, was unable to defend the land because he did not have enough weapons, soldiers, or the support of the Dutch colonists. He had no choice but to surrender to the English troops.

After King Charles II claimed victory over the Dutch, he gave New Netherland to his brother James, the Duke of York. James, who later became King James II, changed the name of the colony from New Netherland to New York.

Peter Stuyvesant

# New Jersey

**First Settlements Established**
1660

**Type of Colony**
Proprietary; Later Royal

**Leaders**
John Berkeley and
George Carteret

**Did You Know?**
New Jersey was named in honor
of his friend Sir George Carteret.
Carteret had been governor of
Jersey, which is an island in the
English Channel. Jersey had been
loyal to the king during the
English Civil War.

The Dutch and Swedish were the first Europeans to settle the land now known as New Jersey. After England claimed victory over the Dutch in 1664, the Duke of York gave a portion of this large area of land to two of his friends. Lord John Berkeley and Sir George Carteret.

English colonists arrived to establish the New Jersey settlements. The English took over an area previously claimed by Dutch and Swedish settlers.

An early New Jersey farm

Berkeley and Carteret had authority over the land and were given permission to divide the region or rent it to others. Berkeley and Carteret established laws for the colony, although they still had to obey English law. They allowed the settlers to practice any religion freely, which made the colony very appealing to settlers.

In 1674 a religious group called Quakers bought a portion of New Jersey from Berkeley. The colony was divided into West Jersey and East Jersey. West Jersey became the first Quaker colony in America. Eventually England reclaimed all of the land to make New Jersey a single royal colony.

# Pennsylvania

**First Settlements Established**
1682

**Type of Colony**
Chartered

**Leader**
William Penn

**Did You Know?**
William Penn first named the colony *Sylvania*, which means "woods." King Charles II of England added "Penn" to the beginning of the colony's name to honor Penn's father.

The Quakers living in England were often **persecuted** because of their religious beliefs. William Penn was a Quaker who was arrested many times because he refused to join the Church of England. Penn was also sent home from college because he refused to attend prayer sessions.

Although Penn was very outspoken, King Charles II liked him – Penn's father had previously let the king borrow money. In 1681 after the elder Penn died, King Charles II repaid his debt by providing William with a charter to establish a settlement in North America. This land would later become the colony of Pennsylvania.

William Penn

## The Quakers

The Quakers were very different from other religious groups in England. They believed that all people were equal — men and women, kings and commoners, the rich and the poor. They allowed women to speak publicly on social issues. Quakers also spoke against war and refused to serve in the army.

Penn was named the colony's governor, and Pennsylvania became a safe place for Quakers to settle. People from many different religions flocked to Pennsylvania because Penn promised religious freedom for all.

Penn returned to England in 1684. While he was away, the leaders who were left in charge of the Pennsylvania colony began to argue over questions of government. This unrest continued until 1699, when Penn returned. In 1701 he reduced the size of the government and gave more power to the colonists.

# Delaware

**First Settlements Established**
1638

**Type of Colony**
Proprietary

**Leader**
William Penn

**Did You Know?**
In 1610 Captain Samuel Argall sailed from the Virginia colony to cross the Atlantic Ocean. A storm threatened his journey, and his ship was pushed off course. He entered a bay, which he later named Delaware (in honor of Lord de la Warr, the governor of Virginia). The Delaware colony was established near the bay.

Delaware's history is linked to Pennsylvania. The Swedish first settled in the area in 1638 and called their settlement New Sweden. After the English seized New Sweden in 1664, the leaders of New York governed the settlement until 1682.

William Penn wanted the Pennsylvania Colony to have a direct passageway to the Atlantic Ocean. The Duke of York decided to give Penn New Sweden in 1682.

This area of land was called Pennsylvania's Lower Counties. As Pennsylvania grew, the colonists living in the Lower Counties feared they would no longer have an equal say in matters of government. They did not feel comfortable sending their leaders to meetings in Philadelphia. In 1701 the colonists asked Penn if they could form their own government. He agreed but demanded that the Lower Counties remain under the guidance of the Pennsylvania governor.

# Chapter 4

# The Chesapeake Colonies

The English settlers at Roanoke had been unfamiliar with the new land as well as the climate. The land was swampy, and temperatures were hot in the summer and freezing in the winter. To complicate matters, the settlers were unable to effectively communicate with the Native Americans.

Eventually the English successfully established two settlements near Roanoke along the Chesapeake Bay. The two colonies would be called Virginia and Maryland.

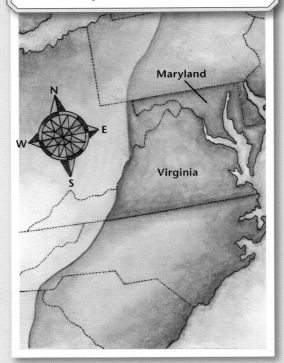

**Chesapeake Colonies**

# Virginia

**First Settlements Established**
1607

**Type of Colony**
Seeking gold

**Leader**
John Smith

**Did You Know?**

Jamestown was named in honor of King James I.

Following the failed attempts to establish the Roanoke colony, in 1606 King James I gave the Virginia Company of London a proprietary charter to establish the colony of Virginia. The Virginia Company wanted colonists to find gold in America and ship it back to England. Later that year about 100 people sailed for Virginia. Upon reaching the Chesapeake Bay, they founded the first permanent English settlement in Virginia, which they called Jamestown.

The Virginia Company expected the settlers to find plenty of gold, and to help make this happen they instructed the colonists to maintain good relations with the Native Americans. The company provided goods such as axes, shovels, and blankets to be traded to the Native Americans in exchange for corn. In order to keep tight control over what they thought would be a moneymaking operation, the Virginia Company appointed a group of overseers led by Captain John Smith.

John Smith, an English soldier, sailor, and adventurer, was the stern leader of the Jamestown settlement.

## A Rough Start

Due to the very harsh weather and living conditions, the Jamestown settlement had many problems. Most of the area was swampland that was full of mosquitoes, and these insects spread diseases such as **malaria** among the settlers.

Unfortunately, the original settlers neither discovered gold nor quickly mastered the hunting or farming skills necessary to acquire food. Many Jamestown settlers died because they were unprepared for such a rugged environment.

Ships arrive from England to relieve the Jamestown settlers.

Visitors today can see a reconstruction of the Jamestown settlement.

As living conditions worsened in the Jamestown settlement, Smith and the other leaders focused their efforts on surviving rather than finding gold. In 1608 Smith demanded that the colonists work hard and learn the hunting and farming skills necessary to survive. In order to improve relations with the Native Americans, Smith worked with Powhatan, the most powerful Native American chief in the area.

The Jamestown settlement began to prosper until 1609, when Smith returned to London because he was wounded in a gunpowder explosion. The following winter was very severe, and it was difficult to find food; many settlers died because of **famine**. This period is known as the Starving Time. People ate dogs, cats, rabbits, and mice in order to survive.

In the spring many settlers decided to return to England. As they were heading back, they met up with additional ships that were heading toward the Virginia colony. Lord de la Warr, who was appointed as the new governor of the Virginia colony, was on board one of the ships. The ships carried additional settlers and supplies. At the sight of Lord de la Warr and the vast amount of supplies on board, the settlers who had been heading to England decided to turn around and go stay in Virginia.

Lord de la Warr

Like Smith, Lord de la Warr demanded that the colonists work hard in order to settle the area. When the settlers learned to grow tobacco in 1612, life began to improve. They sold the tobacco to Native Americans and back in England for a large profit. Under the leadership of de la Warr, Virginia grew to become a well-established colony.

## Pocahontas

Many stories have been written about Pocahontas, who was born in 1596. She was the daughter of Powhatan, a very powerful Native American chief. Pocahontas was actually the nickname of this famous Native American; her real name was Matoaka. Her marriage to English colonist John Rolfe helped create peace between the colonists and Native Americans.

In 1624 King James I cancelled the Virginia Company's charter because the colony had been run poorly and the colonists dealt with the Native Americans badly. Virginia became the first royal English colony. Now the colony was under direct control of the king, and he sent royal governors to rule for him. By 1642 England had established several different settlements in the region as well as a strong colonial government.

King James I

The following is a paraphrased **memoir** from George Percy, an early Jamestown colonist. In the memoir, Percy recounts the horrible conditions that he and the other colonists experienced during the first year in the Jamestown settlement.

*Our men have been destroyed by fever and wars. Many have died from starvation. Englishmen have never been left in a foreign country in such misery. There is little food. Several men are forced to share one can of barley each day. We have no choice but to drink cold river water, which is filled with slime and filth.*

The colony of Jamestown, Virginia was established successfully only after several years of hardship.

# Maryland

**First Settlement Established**
1634

**Type of Colony**
Royal

**Leader**
Cecilius Calvert

**Did You Know?**
Maryland was named for Henrietta Maria, the wife of Charles I.

In 1632 George Calvert, also known as the first Lord Baltimore, was very unhappy in his homeland of England. During this time, most people in England considered themselves Puritans. Puritanism had become a major religion in England in the early 17th century. Calvert, however, was not a Puritan, and he believed in religious freedom. Many people in England were imprisoned or even killed if they practiced the wrong religion. George Calvert didn't lose his life, but many people disliked him. After visiting the Jamestown settlement, he decided to begin a colony where people could enjoy religious freedom.

Cecilius Calvert, the second Lord Baltimore, took over for his father and established the Maryland colony.

The settlers in the Chesapeake colonies tried to maintain good relationships with Native Americans.

Later that year, King Charles I provided Calvert with a charter to establish the large colony of Maryland. Today this area includes parts of the states of Maryland, Delaware, Virginia, Pennsylvania, and West Virginia. Unfortunately, Calvert died before he could establish the colony, so King Charles reassigned the charter to George's son, Cecilius, the second Lord Baltimore. In 1634 the young Calvert sent more than 200 settlers to begin the colony.

The settlers who founded Maryland had heard about the mistakes the Virginia settlers had made in Jamestown, so the new settlers decided to do things differently.

The Maryland settlers established peace with the Native Americans early on and built their first settlement on land that was purchased from the Yaocomico tribe. They named the first Maryland settlement St. Mary's City. Many of the Maryland colonists became very wealthy by farming and selling various crops.

The Maryland colonists learned from the mistakes of previous colonists. Their settlements prospered.

# Fight for Freedom

Cecilius Calvert never settled in Maryland. He stayed in England and collected the money that came from his colony. He appointed his brother Leonard as **governor** of the colony. The Calverts were considered good leaders by many of the colonists because they insisted that the settlers play a role in Maryland's government. In 1649 Maryland's government passed a **revolutionary** law called the Act of Religious Toleration, which allowed colonists to practice any religion. After the law was passed, Maryland became well known among the other colonies for supporting religious freedom. As a result, many new colonists moved to Maryland.

While Maryland had different leaders over the years, the Calvert family controlled the colony until 1775.

## Childhood in the Colonies

There were many children in the colonies who were required to work and go to school just like everyone else—but they also had time for some fun! Colonial children had parks in their communities, but they didn't have playgrounds or swing sets. Parks were called the commons, which is short for common area. Children played games such as tag, marbles, hide-and-seek, and hopscotch. They also made their own kites to fly.

# Chapter 5

# The Southern Colonies

The Southern Colonies include North Carolina, South Carolina, and Georgia. Although the colonies are often grouped together, they each have very distinct histories.

The states of North Carolina and South Carolina were once a single colony called Carolina. Georgia was settled in part as a shield between the Spanish in Florida and the wealthy farmers in South Carolina.

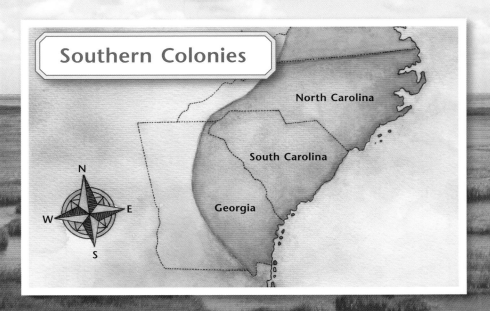

**Southern Colonies**

North Carolina

South Carolina

Georgia

N
E
W
S

# South Carolina

**First Settlement Established**
Carolina: 1663
South Carolina: 1712

**Type of Colony**
Proprietary

**Leaders**
Eight different English investors

**Did You Know?**
Before the English arrived, South Carolina had been part of the Spanish province of Florida.

In 1629 King Charles I gave Sir Robert Heath land in North America, which Heath called Carolina. This area included what are today the states of North Carolina and South Carolina.

## Proprietors in Charge

Heath never established any settlements in the area, so the king chartered the land to eight lord **proprietors**. The eight men did not live on the land and instead used this charter as an investment opportunity.

In 1669 the proprietors sent settlers to Carolina. They set up the colony's first permanent settlement, Charles Town, which was later shortened to Charleston.

Charles Town

The proprietors controlled Carolina until 1719. However, they did not protect the colonists from attacks by the French or Native Americans. Carolina became a royal colony, and King George II provided the settlers with better protection and more religious freedom. Many settlers came from Barbados, an English colony in the Caribbean, and colonized Carolina.

## Olaudah Equiano

Olaudah Equiano was born in 1745. When he was eleven years old, he was taken from his family in Africa. He was forced to board a ship headed for Barbados in the West Indies. Olaudah was frightened; he didn't have anyone to talk to because no one spoke his language. He was later sent to work as a slave in the American colonies.

Equino learned to read and write, and later he wrote a story about his life. His book helped people understand how slavery was wrong.

## Rich in Rice

According to some historians, the Africans who were brought to Carolina knew a lot about farming. Many believe that the African Americans in the area were responsible for discovering that rice could grow well in the swampland near the Atlantic coast.

## *Growing Rice*

In 1685 a group of farmers discovered that rice could grow well in the swampland of Carolina. Soon colonists began growing and exporting rice throughout the world. However, the colonists needed additional help because of the amount of work required to harvest the rice. The colonists from Barbados had previously used slaves from Africa and decided to use this system of forced labor in the rice fields of Carolina.

Before long there were more African Americans in the southern portion of Carolina than white colonists. The region quickly became an **aristocracy**: a few people in the area were wealthy landowners and demanded that slaves do all the work.

# North Carolina

**First Settlement Established**
Carolina: 1663
North Carolina: 1712

**Type of Colony**
Proprietary; Later royal

**Leaders**
Eight lord proprietors

**What's in a Name?**
Carolina was named in honor of King Charles I. *Carolus* is the Latin form of the name Charles. "North" was later added to the name after the land was divided and renamed as North and South Carolina.

Because North Carolina and South Carolina started out as one territory, both colonies share some of the same history. As different Europeans began establishing settlements in the area, however, the two regions began to grow and develop very differently.

For years Carolina was divided into sections that were called counties with a different governor assigned to each one. Eventually, the northern portion of Carolina became a single county. Many colonists living in the north were not happy with the way Carolina was governed. Some believed that the colonists living in the south received more attention because of the amount of wealth they had gathered by growing and exporting rice.

In 1712 after several years of conflict, the land was divided into North Carolina and South Carolina. Different settlements began to appear in many locations along the Atlantic coast and at the mouths of rivers.

In 1729 England established North Carolina as a royal colony. Farmers realized the value of growing tobacco, and the colony became a success.

The economy of the North Carolina colony depended largely on the growth of tobacco.

# Georgia

**First Settlement Established**
1732

**Type of Colony**
Proprietary

**Leader**
James Edward Oglethorpe

**What's In a Name?**
Georgia was named in honor of England's King George II.

The history of the Georgia colony is linked to the colonizing of Carolina as well as Florida. England was responsible for colonizing North and South Carolina. This land, however, was not too far from Florida, which was under Spanish control. The Spanish settlers worked very hard to protect their land and would battle anyone they believed might challenge their rule.

## A Colony of Debtors

In 1732 King George II of England granted a charter to establish the colony of Georgia. He believed that a buffer between Florida and the wealthy colonists of South Carolina was necessary. The land between the two areas was ideal. The king named James Edward Oglethorpe as the leader of the new colony.

Because Oglethorpe was unhappy with the way England treated its poorer citizens, he wanted to establish a colony that would support the **impoverished** people in his homeland. Oglethorpe was also unhappy with how English rulers abused people who owed money; those who owed the government were often arrested and imprisoned. Oglethorpe questioned how someone in prison could pay a debt. He suggested that people be allowed pay their debts by working in the new colony of Georgia.

Georgia's first settlement was the town of Savannah. Oglethorpe managed the colony and made several rules. He wanted the colonists to live on small farms instead of large plantations and did not allow them to use enslaved people to do their work.

The colonists, however, did not like these rules. Eventually the colonists were able to remove Oglethorpe from power, and he was forced to leave the colony. King George II chartered Georgia as a royal colony in 1752.

James Edward Ogelthorpe

# Chapter 6

# A New Nation

As the English colonies in North America continued to grow and prosper, many colonists began to believe that they should have a greater voice in their own government. Citizens in England elected representatives who worked with the king to make and enforce the laws, but American colonists were expected to obey these laws without being able to elect anyone to speak for them. In some cases, American colonists were required to obey stricter laws than their English cousins.

Some people insisted that the American colonies must be completely free from English rule. These people, from all thirteen colonies, began to meet secretly in homes and churches to discuss their ideas. Other colonists began to disobey certain laws openly.

When English authorities saw the laws being broken and found out about the secret meetings, they asked the king to send soldiers to the colonies. When English troops arrived, many colonists became even angrier. Soon a large number of American colonists joined together to protect their businesses, farms, and families from the soldiers. In the spring of 1775, colonists and English troops met in battle for the first time.

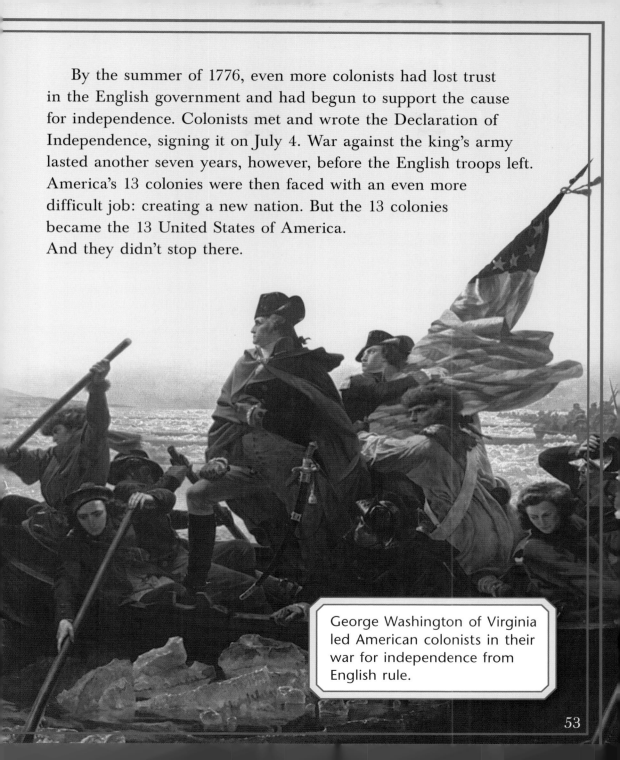

By the summer of 1776, even more colonists had lost trust in the English government and had begun to support the cause for independence. Colonists met and wrote the Declaration of Independence, signing it on July 4. War against the king's army lasted another seven years, however, before the English troops left. America's 13 colonies were then faced with an even more difficult job: creating a new nation. But the 13 colonies became the 13 United States of America.
And they didn't stop there.

George Washington of Virginia led American colonists in their war for independence from English rule.

# A Colonial Time Line

**1490**

**1492** Columbus lands near North America

**1600**

**1607** English colonists settle Jamestown, Virginia

**1620** Pilgrims establish the Plymouth Colony

**1620**

**1630** Puritans establish the Massachusetts Bay Colony

**1623** John Mason and Sir Ferdinando Gorges establish the first settlements of New Hampshire

**1640**

**1634** Cecilius Calvert establishes a settlement in Maryland

**1626** Peter Minuit purchases Manhattan Island from Native Americans

**1636** Settlers establish first colony in Connecticut

**1660**

**1636** Roger Williams establishes Rhode Island

**1680**

**1660** New Jersey is established

**1682** William Penn establishes the Pennsylvania Colony

**1663** Carolina Colony established

**1700**

**1712** Carolina is divided between North Carolina and South Carolina

**1733** Oglethorpe establishes Georgia Colony

**1720**

**1740**

# Glossary

**aristocracy** region ruled by a small group of very wealthy people

**charter** legal document that gives certain rights

**colonies** areas ruled by another country

**expeditions** long journeys or voyages for the purpose of exploring new or unknown territories

**exported** sent outside a country for sale in another country

**famine** severe shortage of food that may result in starvation

**governor** appointed or elected leader of a colony or state

**impoverished** made poor

**malaria** deadly disease caused by microorganisms spread by mosquitoes

**memoir** description of experiences told or written from memory

**persecuted** have one's rights taken away, be abused

**proprietors** people who begin and operate a business

**proprietary** having to do with property and business

**royal** from or belonging to a king or queen

**revolutionary** causing a major change

**tolerance** accepting the rights, beliefs, and customs of others

# Index